I0082368

Unprosecuted

Eric Garrett

Genius
Book Publishing

Los Angeles, California

Unprosecuted
Copyright © 2020 Eric Garrett

All Rights Reserved. No part of this book may be reproduced by any means without the written permission of the publisher, except for short passages used in critical reviews.

While every effort has been made to ensure the accuracy of this information, some names have been changed to protect the identity of witnesses. When real names have been used, they are a matter of public record.

Published by:
Genius Book Publishing
31858 Castaic Road, 154, Castaic, CA 91384
GeniusBookPublishing.com

ISBN: 978-1-947521-37-7

200810

In Memoriam

Mary Marshall
September 28, 1933 – July 30, 2020

I will miss her

Prologue

March 25, 1979 was the worst night of my life. That was the night my mother, Paula Garrett, was murdered. I was four years old at the time. The murderer came into her bedroom and killed her in front of me. I was beaten with the same blunt instrument, and the murderer had every reason to believe he had killed me too. I survived with nine skull fractures and my right side is partially paralyzed. I was lucky that night. She wasn't.

Losing my mother was traumatic enough. The second worst part is that for my whole life I've been told that everyone knows who committed the murder. A suspect was quickly arrested. He wasn't the only suspect at first; in the early days, others were investigated and eliminated. On April 12, 1979, The [Muncie Indiana] Star Press's headline read "Murder Suspect List Narrowed to 1." The prosecutor, Michael "Mick" Alexander, called it an open-and-shut case.

Something happened before the trial could start, though no one is willing to talk about what it was. Just as the case was going to trial, Mick Alexander declined to prosecute. He dismissed the charges on the grounds there was insufficient evidence. Everyone wanted to know, how did a sure thing suddenly lack evidence? In that same April article, The Star Press reported that "Part of the evidence police have gathered from [our] home includes 27 bags of blood-stained articles which have been sent to a police laboratory. Included were scrapings of flesh and hair taken from the fingernails of the victims and the suspect." Since that time, the 27 bags of evidence were "destroyed in a flood" in a police evidence room; a flood that no one remembers and that damaged no other evidence.

In a world where authorities do their jobs and criminals are brought to justice, this case would have been closed decades ago. But at this time the Muncie Police consider the case "open." The status of being an "ongoing investigation" means that none of the evidence, records, or interviews can be released to the public or our family. The official word from the Muncie Police is that this case is unsolved.

The problem with that logic is simple. Everyone knew at the time of the murder who did it. There were at least five actual witnesses, including me. That hasn't changed in forty years. There never was a lack of evidence, though much of it was inconvenient, at least for those who had reason to make this whole thing go away. This case isn't unsolved. It is unprosecuted.

Other people have died in connection with this murder. And yet, shortly after the murder, the man who I and many other people believe to be my mother's killer had a lucrative government contract to rebuild the sewer in the neighborhood where I was living, right outside my aunt and uncle's door. I could see the trucks with his name on them not fifty feet from the living room window. The connections that helped get him out of the murder charges were making him rich. And free. But more on that later.

My mother was murdered, and the man who "everyone knew" did it lives down the road from me even today. I see him from time to time. This same man beat a four-year-old child with a blunt object so badly as to cause lifelong damage. The fact that he didn't succeed in killing me must have been as big a surprise to him as the fact that he never went to prison for the murder surprises me and my family.

I'm not going to prove a case against the killer in this book. If I had access to the evidence the police have, I would spend every penny I have to hire a lawyer to take that man to court to make him face what he did. A lot of what I know and what I've learned from those who were there is contradictory. I'm leaving it up to you, the reader, to draw your own conclusion about what happened. It's less than I want—I *want* a conviction—but it may be all I can hope for.

Paula Garrett was 22 years old the day she died. She never had a chance at life because she was beaten to death. Forty years later, I want her to have the chance to have her short life known. I want the murderer to have to face his actions. And I want to expose the people who protected him then, and are protecting him now.

This book is my attempt to achieve those goals.

6

Paula

I grew up hearing stories of my mother from my grandmother and aunts. They are just snapshots of a life, but they are all I have. Like one time, when Paula was about three years old, they took her to a park with a lake or a big pond (my grandmother Mary would change the details from time to time). Mary took her eyes off Paula for just a moment, and off she ran, right down the dock and straight into the water. "We simply had to jump in after her," Mary said. "She was a real handful. You had to watch her all the time."

Once when I was preparing this book, my grandmother told me, "Her dad went out the front door for something. It was after dark. He didn't shut the door tight. And I was in the kitchen. And so [Paula] went out the front door and was gone. I had no idea where she was. When I missed her, I went outside, but I couldn't see anything. I had to get in the car and drive around trying to find her. I had a sister, Jane, who lived nearby. You could go to her house if you went out my back kitchen door and across three or four yards to her backyard. Jane wasn't home and here come Paula down Jane's driveway. She was a handful."

Paula was born April 4, 1956, the third of five children. Susy was the oldest. There was a brother, Michael, who died from a problem with his heart when he was only three months old. Paula came next, and she was about 18 months older than her sister Lisa. Since they were so close in age, Paula had a special bond with Lisa. The youngest was Molly.

Mary tells of the time that Paula, only about three years old, got into the candy jar, and of course she wanted to share the candy with her sister Lisa.

So she jumped into 18-month-old Lisa's bed and shared a chocolate bar. When Mary found them, Lisa was covered in chocolate, and Paula had a fair amount on her as well. I would say that was her age, but my grandma says it was her intelligence and her accompanying lack of sense.

This would play out with her and my father, Ronnie, and later with the man who would end her life.

"She adored her dad [Fred]," my grandmother tells me. "And he was never there. He finally left me there with four little girls. That was really hard on Paula." When asked, Susy said that when Fred left, "It seemed to affect Paula a lot. She was a daddy's girl, pretty much. But I don't remember him being there." Lisa said of her father, "We weren't close. I don't know if it was just how things were done back then. You divorced the wife and you divorced the family." Fred was an alcoholic, the kind of guy who would just go off and do his own thing. He would leave and be gone for weeks at a time. Lisa added, "When the divorce and all that came [when I was] a young kid, it wasn't that big of a difference because he wasn't home much anyway. I only saw him once in a while. Him being gone all the time, I don't remember it affecting me, which Mom says that it did. It was more of an impact for Paula and Susy."

According to Mary, "Paula was scary smart. She excelled in almost every subject in every grade." The way Mary tells it, Paula took Latin in middle school but struggled with calculus in tenth grade. However, as Paula's teacher explained, "she was only a tenth grader and everyone else in the class were seniors. It was to be expected for her to have a bit of trouble."

When asked if Paula was mature, Mary said, "Oh, yes, but she didn't have a lot of common sense. I've seen that so many times with kids who were smart." My aunts Molly and Susy called her a "Brainiac, but not so smart when it came to men." Paula met Ronnie Garrett in high school. He was two years older, and they dated for a while. By her senior year, she was pregnant with me. According to my aunts, being pregnant in school in the 1970s "wasn't really that uncommon. So it wasn't that much of a stigma." Understandably, being pregnant in her senior year put a damper on her life. Paula attended the local "career center," a kind of vocational or technical school, for her senior year. It was for students who weren't going to go to college.

Paula and Ronnie got married right before I was born. According to Susy, she didn't even know who Ronnie was before they got married. "I had never heard of him. It wasn't as though he was coming to the house or anything." Molly agreed. Ronnie "didn't come around a lot. He worked second shift. Paula and Eric were always at [Mary's] house. But I didn't see him much and he was usually working or whatever. Drinking. He was a drinker. Causing trouble." Ronnie was not a very nice person, particularly to Paula, and certainly with me growing up. He wasn't abusive— at least, not with me and no one mentioned him hitting Paula—but one thing was clear: Ronnie spent much of his time somewhere else, drinking. My grandfather on Ronnie's side was reportedly abusive to his family and children, which affected Ronnie. Susy knew very little about Ronnie, but she knew that "[Ronnie's] father was horrible. There had been some abuse to Ronnie's mother and him and her siblings. All of that affected Ronnie. He was not the nicest person to Paula. He would stay out and drink. He wasn't abusive—but truthfully, she wouldn't have told me if he was."

Susy recalled something else. "There was a story about a telephone. One night when he was drunk, she hit him with that phone." Paula was no stranger to violence, even just out of high school.

Ronnie and Paula were divorced by the time I was two and a half, when Paula was twenty.

Even though Susy said it, everyone agreed. "[Paula had] really terrible taste in men. When dad was gone permanently after our parents' divorce, Paula was terribly hurt. She was the kind of girl who needed a strong male figure in her life. She would do what dad said, but not anyone else. [After Paula's divorce], she saw a counselor. He agreed she was looking for a father figure."

Susy said, "[Paula] had a very easygoing manner. She didn't have a temper. But she would only listen to [her father]. Well, I think some kids as they're growing up, they're either closer to their mother or their dad. And she would listen to dad. She wasn't disrespectful to our parents. She was a very good kid, she really was."

Molly and Lisa had another memory of Paula. Molly said, "She was friendly, had lots of friends. She was [easy] to get along with. And she was smart, and protective of us [Lisa and Molly]. What I remember was that she was that she was fun loving and really funny. It's hard not to miss that."

I asked my family what Paula was like as a mom. Susy said, "She was a great mom. [You were] the first boy to be in our family. We were a house full of women. [Paula] was crazy over you."

There was no question my mother adored me. My grandmother Mary even said so. But in the same breath, she said, "[Eric] was a handful. So was Paula, but for different reasons. We're talking about a boy and a girl. There's a difference. Paula excelled in every grade in every subject. Eric could have done a lot better than he did. Especially in the earlier grades. Maybe some boys do, but boys don't like school and they don't do as well. Paula was never like that."

Paula started dating Richard Green around the time of her divorce. My family didn't know exactly when she met him. However, Susy told me the story that one time, not long after Paula and

Ronnie were separated, Fred went over to visit Paula and me, and Richard was there at the house, sitting at the kitchen table. This was a surprise to me. I had never heard that story before.

One thing that did become obvious, apart from Paula's poor taste in men, was that she was secretive about her relationships as well, although that wasn't how my family phrased it. Susy felt that Paula didn't want to worry anyone.

Another thing that my family repeated consistently was that Paula would believe anything anyone told her, especially from men. Susy said, "There were things that she told me about Richard, and I'm thinking, are you sure that's right? Are you sure he's telling you the truth? So she would believe, especially men, she would believe everything that Richard told her, just about. I mean, she believed a lot of what he said."

This combination of being a sweet, compassionate, intelligent person who was also a bit gullible and not very smart around men, I believe, was what led to her death at age 22.

Richard Green

No one knows exactly how my mother got mixed up with Richard. There was a suggestion that Paula met him at my Great Aunt Jane's coffee shop, where she and Mary would work from time to time, waiting tables. Richard would come into the coffee shop, so that may have been how they met. But no one could explain how she came to start dating him.

Susy said, "Yeah, that seems to be a big mystery. He was married and had four kids. He's eight years older than me, and I'm six years older than Paula. Figure that one out. Fourteen years. But he was giving her money all the time."

When asked when they first knew about Paula and Richard being together, Molly said, "I knew him from going in the restaurant where Paula and Mom worked, that Aunt Jane owned." Mary, for one, didn't like Richard. At all. "He was just a bastard," Mary said. Actually, none of my family liked him. I don't have any memory of spending time with him before the murder, but afterward I heard from my family that one of the sore spots in Paula's relationship with Richard was that I started acting like him, and not in a good way. No one, particularly my mother, wanted that.

I wanted to know what kind of man Richard was. I asked my grandmother to tell me about him. Mary said, "The only thing I know about him is that he's probably a psychopath and he called Paula 'Dummy.' All the time. 'Hey, Dummy,' he would say. [And,] well, he was a liar. People would say, was he lying? I'd respond, well, was his mouth moving?" She shifted in her chair uncomfortably. "I was one of the only people who would stand up to him. He used to come into the restaurant and I remember one time he did something to Paula's car. I came into work, and he was sitting there, and I headed right for him. Immediately, he was like, 'It's not what you think.' He was on the defensive. I didn't trust him, he was a liar. I knew he was a liar and I told Paula. That poor girl would believe what he said. I said, 'Paula, you can't believe him. He lies.' And of course there were a lot of things that she wouldn't tell me."

Lisa talked about Richard coming into the restaurant where Paula worked. "He was a regular. I used to babysit for Eric while [Paula] was working the third shift. And that's probably how she met him. I knew of him, but not on a personal basis. Like, I didn't know he was married with all those kids. [Jane's restaurant] was all truck drivers who worked for him [Richard]." Which isn't exactly true. According to Susy's husband, Ron—not to be confused with my father, Ronnie—Richard was friends with the truck drivers, but they didn't work for him.

Richard Green, who many people knew as "Dick," worked in a meat processing plant for a while, but his main job was running heavy equipment, like backhoes and cranes. He wasn't particularly successful, and he wasn't terribly rich, but I know he had money because he used to give my mother a lot of it. The effect, which everyone agrees was intentional, was that it made Paula dependent on him, less likely to leave.

Mary said, "[Richard] came in the restaurant all the time. I didn't work nights, and that's when he would usually be in there. Sometimes during the day. I remember he came in one time and Eric happened to be there in the restaurant. I can't remember who brought [Eric] in there. Anyway, Richard and Eric sat next to each other at the counter, which was in the shape of a horseshoe. Eric was trying to talk to him, and Richard was totally ignoring him. And it made me mad. I said, 'Well, he doesn't know any better, Richard. He doesn't know he's supposed to act like he doesn't know you when he's in here.' I said that right to his face. Oh, he was furious with me."

It surprises me that Richard thought that everyone in Muncie didn't know his business. It's a very small town, and everyone knows everyone else's business. Richard thought somehow that didn't apply to him. This included all the affairs he was having on the side of his marriage. As far as I can tell, Paula was just one of the women he was seeing, as well as being married to a woman named Nancy, and raising (or, really, not) their four kids.

Susy described Richard as a "charmer." But my family knew him as a man with no empathy, just a violent, self-centered opportunist. I've since learned that narcissists and psychopaths are like that too. Think about Ted Bundy. All his friends thought he was a great guy. Not so much the women he killed.

"He was a pathological liar," Susy said, "and [Paula] believed everything he said. He came on to her, pursued her. She was a lot younger, very very naïve. He really turned on the charm. And she fell for it."

My aunt Molly went to school with Richard's daughters. "I've heard some stories about Richard abusing his kids. I didn't see it with my own eyes, but I remember in middle school when his daughter [who] was my age, Debbie, was out of school and had to have a monitor [set up] in the class [with a microphone in the classroom and a speaker at home] where she could hear the teacher talking and do her work from home. Richard [had] smashed [Debbie's] hand in the car door. She was out of commission for quite a while."

Lisa confirmed this. "I don't know if he had a [police] record or not, but he had been in trouble with the police before. I mean, one of his own kids was out of school because of him. He shut her hand, slammed it in one of their doors and almost took her off her fingers.... I also heard that he beat his second son, Dave. Almost beat [Dave] to death. His own son. They called the police on [Richard] then."

There was no question that Richard was violent with Paula as well. Susy told me that "one time, she had this horrible place on her head, black and blue on her forehead, down the side of her face. Paula's story was that Richard [had] slammed on the breaks and she hit her head on the dash." [Seatbelts weren't all that popular at that time.] That was suspicious, so I asked Lisa what really happened. Turns out Richard [had] slammed her head into the steering wheel. Lisa said, "I told

Paula, you need to let the police see this, press charges. I asked [Paula] if anything like that had ever happened before, but she denied it. I still didn't get it. Why wouldn't she go to the police? She said, 'He [knows] too many important people uptown. They won't do anything to him.' That made me nervous."

Mary said, "I called the police on him, but the thing of it is, the police had been called on him before. He tried to run over a cop one time. So the cops were kind of scared of him too. The cops knew him. I mean, everybody knew him. And he would say, 'Go ahead and call the police on me. It won't do you no good because I know them all.'"

On at least two occasions Richard tried to run someone off the road. One time, Paula was driving, and a man named John was in the passenger seat. Paula may have been dating him at the time, at or around the same time she was with Richard. Muncie is a small town, and Richard saw them driving together. He ran them down, and Paula had to stop. Richard got out of his car, reached through the window, and slammed Paula's face into the steering wheel, bloodying her face. That may have been the time Susy talked about, but it probably wasn't.

Molly told of several times she saw Richard being violent with Paula. "I saw him. I babysat for Eric many times and saw the abuse with my own eyes. But I was the little sister and Paula would tell me, 'Don't tell mom.' So I didn't. I did threaten to call the police a couple of times [when] he was outside, shaking her around like a rag doll, and I could hear the commotion. I opened the door and said I'm going to call the police. I was about 13 or 14 at the time. Paula would defend him. 'Don't do that,' she'd say. 'You'll get me kicked out [of my rental house].' I never called the cops, but I said if Richard didn't leave I would. Then he would leave."

Everyone agreed that Paula wasn't Richard's only affair. Susy said, "He was a womanizing horn-dog." My family said that he was probably having three or four affairs at that time, and didn't care if anyone knew it. His wife was loyal to him—more than likely for the same reason Paula was—and she wasn't going to leave him over some affairs. So he was screwing everyone, including Paula. It was a wonder he was ever home to abuse his children. Mary said, "[Paula] wasn't the only girlfriend he had. One was a high school girl." Richard was about 35 or 36 at the time this was all going on, around the time of the murder. "She [the girl] got away from him, but he would still pester her. When she went out with some other guy, Richard showed up. She said, 'Run. He'll kill you.' He even tried to go out with me [Mary]. And I was older than him."

"Richard was a very violent person. And Eric began mimicking him in talk and behavior. Eric really liked Richard. That concerned everyone, especially Mom and Paula," Susy said. "As Eric got older, you couldn't take him anywhere. He was out of control." Billy, Lisa's husband, said, "Richard was a bad influence on Eric. He did terrible things, shouldn't have been around Eric. That's where Eric got a lot of his attitude at that time. It was mostly language. [Richard] never hit Eric, but he would do mean, terrible things in front of him. It rubbed off on [Eric], who would imitate Richard. [Eric] walked like [Richard]. They were together all the time. Eric's mouth was terrible. He got it from Richard. Eric called me a son of a bitch when we were shopping in a mall and I said 'we're outta here.' Four-year-old calling me names. That was the influence Richard had over [Eric]."

Susy said that was part of the reason Paula decided to get away from Richard. I can only imagine other reasons were the violence, the lies. All of it.

When Paula finally tried to get away from Richard, he didn't like that at all. He wouldn't let her go. He started following her, stalking her. He would sneak up to our house and look in the windows. Susy said, "There was one night I remember. We were at her house talking. She said, be quiet, don't talk so loud. The windows were open. Richard might [have been] out there listening to our conversation! They didn't have stalking or domestic abuse laws back then. It just wasn't talked about. I told Paula, 'I don't think he's going to leave you.' Paula started getting really frightened. She tried to get her courage up to call Richard's wife, Nancy, get her to get Richard to leave [her] alone. I told her not to go about it that way. See, Richard was giving Paula money, making her depend on him. Richard was scared she was really going to leave him. And Paula was getting upset about the changes in Eric's behavior. Paula meant business this time, trying to get away from him. Richard knew it, too."

I want to note something here. According to noted prison psychologist Dr. Al Carlisle, author of *Violent Mind: The 1976 Psychological Assessment of Ted Bundy* and *The Mind of the Devil: The Cases of Arthur Gary Bishop and Westley Allan Dodd*, "psychopath" is not a diagnosis, it is a description, same with "sociopath." You won't find "psychopath" in the *Diagnostic and Statistical Manual V* (DSM V), a reference guide for psychiatric professionals on diagnosing mental disorders. The closest thing to a diagnosis like that is Antisocial Personality Disorder, which appears in the DSM V. But that doesn't mean that psychopath is not a useful term. And it is very descriptive here. I don't know if Richard was ever diagnosed with Antisocial Personality Disorder— I'm not a psychiatrist and don't have access to his medical records—but calling him a psychopath is an accurate description.

This is what a psychopath looks like (according to Dr. Al Carlisle):

1. Overconfidence and extreme narcissism
2. Shallow, superficial emotions
3. Insincerity and constant (pathological) lying
4. Callousness and lack of guilt, remorse, or empathy
5. Manipulative and selfish
6. Impulsiveness and constant need for stimulation
7. Promiscuous sexual behavior
8. Delinquency and behavior problems early in life
9. Lack of realistic long-term goals (the key here is "realistic")
10. Irresponsibility and tendency to blame others
11. Criminal acts (may not be caught or convicted)

Does that remind you of anyone here?

The Murder

It shouldn't be a surprise at this point that the number one suspect in the murder of my mother was Richard Green. He was a violent, abusive asshole—and given the fact that he tried to run over a police officer as well as my family, it is not too much of a stretch to conclude that he wasn't above murder.

To be fair, this is still the United States of America, and there is still a presumption of innocence until someone is proven guilty in a court of law. This book isn't court. I'm not a lawyer, and this isn't a prosecution. The case is still considered "open" by the police, so I don't have access to the evidence for or against Richard Green. The police and the prosecutor, Mick Alexander— who, by the way, is dead—have it, and so does Richard's family—they were entitled to know the prosecution's case against Richard, which included the bloody crime scene photographs and basically everything they won't share with me and my family—and they have decided there is not enough evidence to prosecute Richard. But I'm getting ahead of myself.

There are only two people alive who were in the room when the murder took place, me and Richard Green, and Richard isn't talking. As a four-year-old with nine skull fractures, I don't really have a good memory of the events of that night. I know that back in those days, I would sometimes get up in the middle of the night and get into bed with my mom. I was in her bedroom when Richard came in and started fighting with my mom, so apparently I had in fact gone into my mom's bedroom that night. I have one more flash of memory that I know is true. I remember being wakened up by the light coming on, and Richard was there and he had something in his hand. That's all I can consciously remember about that night. Part of me wishes I remembered more. However, if the nightmares I have give me any idea of what it would be like to have a complete memory of that night, maybe it's better that I have blocked it out.

But I will tell you this. My uncle on my father's side, Muncie Police Officer Donny Garrett, interviewed me after I was out of the hospital. The interview was videotaped. When asked who hurt me, I said, "Richard... Richard Green." I also picked him out of a picture lineup of ten photos. Some people, particularly those who don't want to see Richard prosecuted for my mother's murder, think I was an unreliable witness. After all, what the hell does a four-year-old know? But I know that Richard was the one who murdered my mother. I saw him in the room that very night it happened. You don't forget something like that.

I want to tell you that my publisher gave me a hard time about me "knowing" Richard did it. Witnesses can be and are often wrong about what they see and hear during crimes. But I want to say something about that. I was sure it was Richard when I was four years old, and I'm sure now. I was there.

Witnesses to the Murder

There were four witnesses other than me who have something to contribute to putting the story of that night together. I've changed their names but not what they told me.

Harry

Harry was 18 years old on the night of the murder. He worked at a local McDonald's, perhaps five minutes from the red brick duplex where Paula and I lived on the corner of Primrose Lane and Azalea Lane in Yorktown, next to Muncie. He lived in the house on the other side of our duplex, on the right side from the street.

McDonald's closed at 11 o'clock in those days, and Harry had to stay to clean up until midnight or 12:30am. He came home a short time after that and saw Richard Green walking toward my house. Harry recognized him and said something like, "Hey, how are you doing?" But Richard didn't say anything to him, just kept walking. Harry didn't think too much about this until he heard about the murder a day or two later.

On May 23, 1979, eight days after Richard was taken into custody, there was a bond hearing for Richard, and Harry was a witness. He pointed Richard out in the courtroom and said that he saw Richard hurriedly walking away from Paula's house around 3am on the night of the murder. I want to point out that that would be three hours after Harry saw Richard the first time. What Harry was doing out at 3am is anyone's guess. Regardless, based on that, and I'm sure other information, Judge Steven Caldemeyer ruled at the time that Richard could not be released on bond.

Not long after the murder, Harry started getting death threats. On August 29, 1979, the Muncie Evening Press reported that "one witness who previously testified at a court hearing that he had seen Green walking in the neighborhood of Mrs. Garrett's home on the night of the murder, has since told him [Mick Alexander] he can't remember which night he saw Green." Apparently the witness intimidation was working. His family clearly took the threats seriously because they sent Harry to Texas, where he's been ever since.

In 2015 or so, I tried tracking Harry down to find out what he knows. Before this, I tried calling him but he didn't want to talk. Hardly any of the witnesses wanted to talk because another witness, Pete Journay, was killed—possibly by Richard, probably in connection with my mother's murder, but I really can't say that's the truth because I never found out and that other murder is still "open" as well. More on that later. Anyway, in 2017, Harry's father died, and he came back to Muncie for the funeral. I went over to his mother's house and asked if Harry was there, and he was. He came to the door and I asked if he recognized me. He didn't, which isn't too surprising since the last time he saw me was when I was four years old. He told me the story of what happened and what he saw, and offered to help wherever he could. Like many people I've spoken with, he said, "Everyone knows Richard done it." I've since lost contact with him, so I can't back up this story, but it doesn't matter because there are other witnesses who will back me up, who were willing to talk on the record then, and are still willing to come forward about what they know.

Jonathan

Jonathan is a former Marine, and recently retired from the Palm Beach County (Florida) Sheriff's Office. Jonathan lived in the other part of the duplex my mother and I lived in. Jonathan said, "Our bedrooms were separated by nothing more than a sheet or two of drywall. I could hear everything. Everything.

"Paula was a wonderful girl. Her mother lived right across the street. Paula wanted to be close to her for a variety of reasons." One of those reasons was Richard. "Paula was terrified of Richard. He could go into a rage over the slightest thing. Richard drove a souped-up Ford [pickup] that everyone could hear coming two blocks away. It wasn't like he lived far away, somewhere else. He was right there on the same street. Paula had to pass his porch to get to her mom's house."

It should be noted that this cannot be confirmed. It was widely reported in the papers that Richard lived about a mile or a mile and a half from Paula's house—the Muncie Evening Press gave his address in an article on May 16, 1979. So I'm not sure where Jonathan got that Richard lived across the street. However, the papers got a lot wrong, including my age, my mom's age, where I was discovered when the paramedics arrived, and a slew of other facts.

Jonathan continued, "If [Mary] heard him coming and caught [Paula] with him there would be hell to pay."

On the evening of March 24, 1979, Jonathan was home watching television. He was tired that night, and put something on the stereo as he got ready for bed. "I heard Richard's truck pull up [in front of Paula's house]. Heard the door slam. My understanding was that she was in the process of breaking up with him. She was tired of his promises of him leaving his wife. [Paula] had changed the locks on all the doors [to keep Richard out]. So Richard knocks then beats on the door. It was commonplace to hear things torn apart [next door], yelling and screaming." Jonathan chose to stay out of the mess that was brewing that night. "I didn't want to show my face and make things worse for her. I heard a big thud. Later I realized it was Richard kicking the door in. Then there was a bunch of screaming, yelling, some kind of commotion, stuff being thrown around. I could hear [Paula's and Richard's] voices. By this time I think Aaron and had come home with Leslie Ann." Aaron was Jonathan's roommate in those days, and Leslie Ann was a friend of theirs. Aaron and Leslie Ann had been at a local bar that night. "Aaron heard the tail end of the commotion. Then it got quiet and we heard Richard's truck pull away."

Jonathan and Aaron didn't think too much about what was going on next door. It was hardly the first time a fight had happened there.

"The next morning, I got up to get ready to go to work." Jonathan had a construction job building an ice cream shop at the reservoir about eight or ten miles away. "[My boss] asked me sometimes to look around the reservoir, especially the ice cream shop, and see if anyone was stealing anything. I couldn't use my shotgun, so I had gone up to city hall and got an auxiliary ID to carry a handgun, a revolver, in a holster, not concealed.

"As I was getting dressed [that morning], I heard more noise next door, and went into the living room. I zipped up my pants, but didn't have a chance to put my gun and holster on when [the door to my apartment burst open], and there was Richard standing in the living room. My hand went to the gun. We stared at each other for a moment. Richard mumbled something about '[Paula's] really done it this time.' I buckled my pants and wedged myself between Richard and the doorway. Richard told me he had been over at [Mary's] house. [Mary] was [on her way] over to Paula's house."

From what Jonathan recalled, it was pretty clear that Richard wanted to be there when everyone went inside Paula's house, but he needed someone as a witness to give whatever story he told some credibility. That someone was Jonathan. Mary was still on her way.

When Jonathan and Richard got to Paula's door, "Richard and I could see where someone had tried to pry the door open.... We gave it a couple of kicks. We went inside the living room, which looked pretty much in order.

"The first doorway on the right was Paula's room. Eric had a room of his own." Here I have to remind you of something. I had my own room, but after a bad dream that night, my mom had taken me into her room to sleep with her. Jonathan continued: "We turned the corner, and at the threshold of the bedroom we could tell something was wrong. It was a mess. Eric was face down on the floor, unconscious, in a pool of blood. His eyes were closed and he wasn't breathing [as far as we could tell].

"Paula was on the bed in a fetal position. She was pale, white. Her nightgown was pulled up to her waist. I had been a first responder [so I took action]. She was cold, had been dead a while. A window was open, letting in fresh, cold air. There was blood splatter up to the ceiling.

"Richard stayed in the threshold between the bedroom and the living room. He just stared at Paula, and me.

"As soon as I touched Eric he opened his eyes. I told Richard we had to get him out of there. With my left hand I cradled Eric's head, and slipped my right under his waist. I needed Richard to get his feet and ankles to keep him straight and get him into the living room. But Richard refused. He said, 'No, I'm not going in there.' So I managed to get Eric into the living room by myself.

"[Mary] had by now entered the house and was hysterical. I told her to go back to [her] house and call 911. Richard was behaving strangely, kind of humming around the living room. While I was attending to Eric, [Richard] was on the porch a while. About that time, the police and ambulance arrived. I couldn't say where [Mary] was at that point. I accompanied Eric to the hospital in the back of the ambulance. Stayed with him quite a while.

"The investigation… was a circus. Any officer out of the academy could have cleared the case within a few hours. Any attorney in their first year could have prosecuted.

"I spoke to some of the neighbors. They reported that Richard had been peeping that night and the nights before." Here, Jonathan began to speculate. "While beating Paula, Richard didn't plan to kill her. It was a jealous rage. The story went that Paula had found a ride to a local liquor store and had bought a six-pack of beer. A male friend had been over drinking, but Paula hadn't had a beer. [The male friend] had two beers and left empty cans, one in the living room and one in the kitchen. That's how Richard knew someone had been there."

I need to add something here. There is a possibility that the story about having a male friend over drinking beers may not have happened. The beer cans were there, but my aunt Susy reported that Paula may have put them there to make Richard think there had been someone else there. Paula wanted to make Richard think she was seeing someone else, in the hopes that Richard would want to dump her. But it's likely the thing that made Richard boil over. How Paula thought that Richard would just leave her alone goes to show how naïve she really was.

Jonathan continues, "That night [before the murder], when he kicked in the door, he had had a drinking buddy with him, Pete Journay. Pete was an alcoholic. If you bought him a beer, he was your buddy. The story went that Pete was out in the truck when Richard kicked the door in and killed Paula. Not long after the murder, Pete walked in, saw the carnage. Richard [is rumored to have] said, if you shoot your mouth off, the same could happen to you. Well, of course, Pete was in a bar not long afterwards, had a few drinks, and starts shooting his mouth off. About how he was there, saw the blood everywhere. Someone who knew Richard overheard Pete and went to a pay phone to call Richard. So now the phone rings at the bar. It's for Pete. He takes the call, then says, 'I'll be right back. There's someone I'm supposed to meet across the street.' They found [Pete Journay] in the river three days later. This was three weeks before they took Richard Green into custody [for Paula's murder]."

That would put it around the last week of April, 1979, so about four weeks after the murder.

"When Richard was in custody, his cellmate reported that Richard said he didn't do it, but it didn't matter because he wouldn't ever go to trial. He had too much on the 'committee people.'

"There was only one suspect, and everyone knew who it was within minutes of the murder being discovered," Jonathan said. "But Mick Alexander was the prosecutor, and he was looking for an excuse to cut Richard loose."

This next part of Jonathan's account has been confirmed by several others, including the then Deputy Chief of Police, Linda Botkin.

"They gave Richard two polygraphs and he failed both. Mick Alexander's Deputy Prosecutor, Richard Reed, went to school with the chief polygrapher in Chicago three hours away. So two Muncie police detectives drove Richard to Chicago for a third polygraph."

It's more or less common knowledge that polygraph results are inadmissible in court. While we were doing research for this book, my publisher spoke with former Johnson County (Montana) sheriff Paul Redden, who is a well-respected polygrapher who worked in San Diego, California and other places for almost 40 years. What we learned surprised me. Redden said that while the results of the polygraph are inadmissible in court, the interview that takes place during the polygraph examination is completely admissible. Which makes me wonder what happened during the interviews they had with Richard.

Jonathan continued. "It really didn't matter what [Richard] said in the third polygraph examination. He was going to pass. But somehow they forgot to mention to Richard that the fix was in. On the way back from Chicago, they stopped at a restaurant for a bite to eat. They took off Richard's handcuffs so he could use the restroom. Naturally, he went out the window…. [The next day,] Mick Alexander tracked him down and told him that he had passed the third polygraph and it was safe to turn himself in."

The story starts to get weird from here, even though, once again, this was confirmed by many others.

"Mick Alexander also made it public that they had administered a 'truth serum' to Richard." On Wednesday, August 29, 1979, the Muncie Evening Press reported that "Alexander said the results of Monday's test, added to the fact that Green passed a sodium ambutol (truth serum) test, helped lead him to his decision to dismiss the charges." Linda

Botkin said, "That's ridiculous. No defendant would ever be given truth serum, no attorney would ever allow it. It was propaganda to quell public opinion."

"Based on all this theater, they cut Richard loose," Jonathan explained.

"As the years have gone by, people have tried to delve into this case. [Because the case is 'open,'] others have tried and failed to get their hands on the physical evidence to re-examine it. The Muncie police have been slow to walk it [work on it], making stupid excuses. They claim there was a flood in the evidence room that destroyed the evidence from this case only." This story, that there was allegedly a flood no one remembers, has also been confirmed by others. "The evidence room is one of the most secure places on earth. But somehow the evidence was lost," Jonathan said. I wasn't one-hundred percent clear on whether Jonathan, as a law enforcement officer, tried to examine the evidence himself, or was speaking about others, but he made it clear that the Muncie police aren't sharing anything. "[We] tried to get information from the state police.

The assistant chief of police, Linda Botkin, was a straight shooter who wound up in a place she really shouldn't have been. She smelled a rat and got her hands on every piece of paper she could, made photocopies. That's as close as anyone has come to seeing the evidence. It's 'still under investigation.'"

Jonathan added, "Five or six years ago, I met with Linda and her family. She gave me a cardboard box with witness statements, etc. I got to look through it, and I put my 30 years of knowledge to it. I poured over it for two days, reports and witness statements both. The evidence is clear.

"It breaks my heart to see Eric go through this. He didn't deserve what happened to him.

"You know, Richard was implicated in three murders." That would be Paula, Pete Journay, and one other. "He killed two or three people but is still walking around because he knows the right people. Every morning, Richard has coffee with four or five retired police officers." I talked to some people in law enforcement—outside of Muncie, outside of Indiana—and asked them why a murder suspect would have coffee with retired police. The answer I got was interesting. Someone is sending a message. The message has some room for interpretation, but one thing is clear. Don't mess with Richard Green unless you want the police department to come down on you as well.

Leslie Ann

Leslie Ann was there that night, around the time of the murder, but she wasn't sure she was in the house when the murder took place. "We [Aaron and I] were there [at Jonathan's side of the duplex] that night, and we'd heard some loud banging going on. I went to ask Jonathan, whose bedroom was back to back with Paula's. I asked what the banging was about, but Jonathan was on a long distance call with someone, a gal in Colorado, and said he would investigate when he was done. I don't think he did check.

"I decided to go on home, and left after a while. When I went out to get my car, there was a guy getting in his truck. He was parked right up in front of [Paula's] house. He seen me coming out. I was going around the left way, which curves onto South Burlington, and he tried to run me off the road. I only lived two or three blocks away on 13th Street. I just thought it was kind of weird that that had happened. I worked at the Pizza King up on 3rd. I was opening one morning, and was there maybe a half hour or an hour, and a detective came in and wanted to sit down and talk. They told me Paula'd been murdered, and Eric had been taken to Indy [Indianapolis] to the hospital. He was there in critical condition. They proceeded to ask me what I heard and seen that night. And I told them 'a silver truck.' I proceeded to tell them that whoever was parked up at the front door came around and tried to run me off the road.

"Few days later I started getting death threats. By then I knew who had done this. Dwayne Cougill was our detective, and he stayed with me for maybe two weeks. At different times, I'd gotten taken up to the detective's office, did hypnosis test on us. I was getting a cold at the time, and once when I was under hypnosis, I coughed and woke myself up. They didn't put me under again. I still always look over my shoulder. The detective, Dwayne Cougill, was friends with my brother-in-law. He told me that he didn't think I had anything to fear because [if Richard did anything] it would incriminate him."

Aaron

Aaron was Jonathan 's roommate at the time of the murder. "I knew Paula, but not real well. Jonathan told me, Paula's boyfriend is crazy, don't mess with him. I could hear them arguing all the time. That night, I got off work and went to the Oasis Bar, and ran into Leslie Ann there. We decided to go to my house and drink some beer. I can tell you when I left the bar, 3:23am minus 7 minutes, which was 3:16am. They hypnotized me at one point and we figured it out.

"So we went to my house, and there's Richard's truck. There's not another one like it, silver, 4-wheel drive. We went inside, put on music, talked, drank beer. Listened to two albums, Kansas and Billy Joel's 52nd Street. I have a photographic memory, and I know cars. We were listening to the music, and about the time we had to change albums, we could hear them arguing. There was a loud noise—I now understand it was the bed breaking—and heard Richard say something to the effect of, 'You think you're going to get away with that?' Once again, Jonathan told me to stay out of it. Went back to Leslie Ann and said, 'Don't worry about it, they do it all the time.'

"Leslie Ann left, and I turned off the music. At one point I went into the bathroom. [The walls were so thin that] I used to mess with Paula. When I heard her in the bathroom, I would say, 'I see you,' and she would laugh. This time there was silence. Later on, I realized it was Richard cleaning up.

"The next day, I had to go to the airport. When I get back, there are cops everywhere, an ambulance. Jonathan told me that Paula had been murdered. They took us downtown to question us. I'm standing in line [waiting to be interviewed], and right beside me is Richard! He asked me, 'What did you see?' I said, 'Your truck.' He denied it. 'Not my truck!'

"[After Richard was arrested,] they denied his bail. Jonathan later told me that he [Richard] had escaped while in Chicago. We called the detectives, 'Have you caught him yet? Did he pass [the polygraph]?' [The detectives said,] 'No, he flunked it.'

"After Chicago, it became an ugly situation. [Richard] told people he would never go to jail for [Paula's murder]. I thought that was strange. Then I'd get phone calls threatening my life. My mom told me if I didn't watch myself I'd end up dead. Cars were following me. Nine days after the murder [actually, it was about a month later], they found a guy [Pete Journay] in the river with similar injuries [blunt force trauma].

"Paula's ex [probably my father, Ronnie, but Aaron wasn't clear] drove a Monte Carlo, and so did Leslie Ann. Richard may have thought that it was the ex he was running off the road.

"I heard Richard say a couple of times, 'I'll never go to jail for that,' meaning Paula's murder. I had a friend who was the biggest drug dealer in Delaware County. He said watch your back, Richard is dangerous. My friend ended up dead. This is hearsay, but I heard that Richard wanted to take over his drug business."

The murder brought Aaron and my aunt Molly together. They married not long after all this happened, and they had two children. Not too long ago, they were divorced.

In addition to the four direct witnesses to the murder mentioned above, my grandmother Mary had something to add to the timeline.

Mary

"March 25, 1979 was the date that the Muncie Central High School, not far from Paula's house, won the state championship. That's a big thing around here. I graduated from there. Hell, everyone did. Well, the doctors' kids went to Burris, and everyone else went to Muncie Central. After the Bear Cats won, Paula called me on the phone. I knew Richard was there that night because I heard him there when I was on the phone with [Paula]. They had been watching the game, or listening to it on the radio, whichever. [Richard] was talking about it, and possibly IU [Indiana University] had been playing that night as well. And [Richard] left because he was going up to the field house [at the high school] because they always have a big celebration [when Muncie Central wins]."

As Jonathan reported, the next morning, Richard had gone over to Mary's house and asked—or told—her to come to Paula's house because "something was wrong." Everyone agrees that this was to establish an alibi, or at least plausible deniability, like he could say, "I didn't know. See, I just saw this for the first time myself." No one believed him. But that's what he did.

I asked what time Richard came to get her [Mary]. She said, "Morning, sometime in the morning. I had been over at my mother's house the night before, and just got home that morning. Richard Green called me on the phone. He said, 'Where's Paula?' And that was the first clue. He never called her Paula. Always 'Dummy.'

"When I got home before he called, I noticed that Paula's car wasn't there. That made me wonder where she was at. But I was tired and wanted a bath, so I didn't think too much about it. Then Richard called, and I told him I didn't know [where Paula was], and I was going to take a bath, and got off the phone. So I get in the bathtub and while I'm in the bathtub [Richard] comes bursting into the bathroom. I mean, I'm in the bathtub stark naked. And he came into my house and right into the bathroom. And I said, 'What are you doing?' And he said, 'Something is wrong with Paula.' And I said, 'What do you mean, something's wrong?' 'Well, she done something to herself.' I said, 'No, she didn't do that. She wouldn't do that.' Then he immediately changes his story to, 'Well, somebody, something happened to her.'"

Mary got out of the bathtub, dressed quickly, and went [across the street] to Paula's house. As Jonathan reported, Richard came to get him, and Mary "was on her way."

Mary said, "They [Richard and Jonathan] go in the front door, and I'm on the porch. They go in and I didn't. Now, who quote-unquote found the body? Well, Jonathan says he did. But I'm thinking [Richard] did originally. I mean, obviously he knew where the bodies were.

"The cops hadn't even been called at this point. She [Paula] was laying on the bed. I think Eric was on the floor beside the bed. Jonathan got in trouble for moving Eric. When Eric opened his eyes, they were blank, there was no expression.

But his face was twitching because they say he was probably having a seizure. Because he had nine skull fractures.

"Paula was gone. I picked up the phone [to call the police], but it was dead. Jonathan told me to go back home and call 911, and I did. They took Eric to the local hospital, and then they drove him in an ambulance to Indianapolis.

"They gave me a shot out there. I can't remember [what happened after] because they gave me the shot [to calm my nerves]. Then I remember later being back home."

"How did you learn about the murder?"

Most of my family found out about the murder shortly after the police arrived. My Great Uncle Phil had the sad duty of calling everyone and letting them know. It didn't take long for my family, and most of Muncie, to find out.

According to Susy, Uncle Phil called her. "I had guests in from Ohio… who came to visit that day. It must have been mid-morning or noon. Uncle Phil asked for Ron [on the phone]. I heard Ron say, 'Oh my God.' That's when I knew something was wrong. Ron got off the phone and said, 'Paula's dead.' Just like that. My daughter remembers me backing up to a wall and sliding down to the floor, and I put my head down. My first thought was, I gotta get to mom. I had two girls. Missy at that time was 10 or 11 years old. Amy was 2 years old. I took the girls to my mother-in-law's house and then went to [find my] my mother [Mary]. I didn't know if Mom could get through this. She looked horrible. They had given her a sedative. I said to her, 'Mom, I don't know why these things happen. This isn't the way for someone to die."

Merle Huffman, who was a suspect for a time, was an old boyfriend of Paula's from middle school. The police interviewed Merle, especially because Richard pointed the finger at him. Richard also pointed the finger at Ronnie, my father. The cops didn't buy it. They were both quickly eliminated as suspects. Richard wasn't.

Susy continued. "Who could do that to a child? Especially if they knew the child. We were all kinda naïve. [After Merle was eliminated as a suspect,] we thought it was some strange nut. The police wouldn't tell us anything. We had to hear it from other people. [Mary's] boyfriend, a man named Von Lamb, was friends with Richard. [Von worked for a company called White Petroleum, and Richard did a lot of backhoe work for them. Von was his immediate supervisor. As time went on,] Von would come back and say, 'it's looking more and more like Richard.' But there still wasn't any concrete evidence on anybody. I kinda gave up on the thought of who could do this. Then things started filtering in about Richard. He beat his wife so severely that he put her in the hospital. He beat his kids. The days went on. It was a nightmare."

Molly remembered, "I had just turned 17, and was still living at home [with my mother, Mary]. I came home and a neighbor came over and said something had happened across the street. Something was wrong. And I went over there [to Paula's] because there were cop cars and all that there. They stopped me from going in and made me go back home. And at that point in time all I knew was that something bad had happened but I didn't know what. It was that evening I found out.

"I was at our apartment and my aunt Jane came over and said we needed to go with her, we needed to go to the hospital, something had happened, but she wouldn't tell me what happened. I knew it was Paula, but she wouldn't tell me anything. [When I got to the hospital] was when I found out. They had my mom in the hospital sitting on a bed, they had given her a sedative. Jane took me out into the hallway and told me about Paula [that she had been hurt, but she didn't say Paula had been killed]. She didn't know about Eric. I went in to see my mom, and she's the one that told me Paula was gone."

The timeline on this next part is a little confused, which seems reasonable. There was a lot going on that day.

Lisa said, "Apparently [Richard] came right into the bathroom while [Mary] was in the tub. I don't think he had been in [Mary's] house before then. At first he said Paula had done something to herself. Mom jumped out of the tub. Then he said, 'Have you checked on Paula yet?' I don't know if he had been back to the scene or not. He tried to get me [Lisa] to go over there. He wanted someone to find her without him. He wanted somebody else to find her. He didn't want to be the one. He called me, 'Where's Dummy? She's not answering her phone.' I told him, 'Well, she's not here.'"

Lisa continued. [Before the police arrived, my boyfriend at the time and I] left and I was going to stop [at Paula's house]. We pulled right up in front of her house, opened the car door. I was going to go up and tell her that 'Richard was trying to find you, Richard's calling.' I looked in front of the house and her car was over to the side. The front door was open. So I thought, well, she's there, she's just not answering her phone. And I shut the car door and left and I didn't go in.

"And then on our way to get something to eat, we're going down to 16th Street and here comes Richard and his truck comes towards us and kind of swerves at us like he's trying to hit us. But we just drove on. I think he was thinking at that time, how is it that nobody has found her yet?

"Paula would have survived if someone had gotten to her [sooner]. That's what we heard, that she bled to death. If somebody had found her and gotten her to the hospital sooner [she might have survived]. It wasn't her injuries necessarily."

When I asked my aunts Molly and Lisa, 'How soon after the murder did everyone know it was

Richard?' Molly was the first to speak. "I knew immediately," she said. "I mean I saw him, I babysat for him many times and I saw the abuse with my own eyes."

Lisa said, "[After the murder,] Richard would come into where I work all the time. Every day. Wanting to know if Eric was talking. 'Has he said anything yet? Is Eric talking? What's he said?' I thought, that's awfully odd. That very night that we went home right after the hospital, he [Richard] was right there. He come up at the table at our house, in the kitchen, and he's asking all kinds of questions right then. And he was trying to throw the blame towards Merle Huffman, an old junior high boyfriend Paula dated off and on. He kept pointing at Merle Huffman. Richard also pointed at Ronnie [Eric's father]. Richard was sucking in that information from us, what we had already found out, and what we'd been talking to the police [about]. We had our suspicions, but it had just happened. In our minds, we were thinking, there was no doubt in my mind that he would do that to her. But Eric threw us. [Richard] wouldn't do that to Eric. You don't do that to someone you supposedly love."

In the Hospital

The next memory I have was waking up in the hospital. They told me I had been in a coma for a couple of days, maybe three days. I couldn't talk for a long time after that. They weren't even certain if I could swallow.

I remember them asking me if I knew where my mom was. They tell me that I said I knew she had gone up to heaven. That was probably later, after I started talking again. That's when the videotaped interview with my uncle Donnie, the policeman, took place. So it was probably right around then.

They didn't know if I was going to live or die. The injuries had caused partial paralysis on my right side, which I still have today. The doctors, everyone, said that I may never walk again, maybe never speak again. But I did. I was talking and running around within a month. I started school the next school year, which was something like four months later.

I asked my grandmother, Mary, what it was like with me in the hospital in Indianapolis, about an hour and a half away in good traffic. She said, "I used to come down there and bring you candy bars. And cereal [probably Fruit Loops, but she wasn't sure]. I brought those things because when I did, they would let me take you out of bed and rock you. The doctors said I could give you anything you wanted because they didn't know if you could swallow or not. Since I could give you anything you wanted, I did."

Susy's husband Ron added, "I understand that Nan and the other grandmother [Ronnie's mother] were staying there by [Eric's] side. I went to the hospital too. When I saw him, [Eric] couldn't even walk. He crawled under the tables. I mean it was just—it was terrible. It's a miracle he's alive. He probably," Ron said, choking up, "by rights he should have—God saved him, I believe that."

Susy was at the hospital visiting a lot too. "Eric was at Indianapolis Methodist Hospital. He came home three weeks later after a miraculous recovery. The emergency room doctors didn't think he'd make it through the ambulance ride to Indianapolis. The neurosurgeon told us that it didn't look good. On the other hand, he [Eric] had one thing on his side, the fact that he was so young. Every day he got better and better. When he came home he still couldn't talk, and couldn't walk very well. He had a limp on his right side and couldn't use his right arm."

I came home to Ron and Susy's house. They had just moved back from Ohio where Ron had been working for Pepsi. My cousins Missy and Amy had a hard time [with me moving in]. But we spent a lot of time together, and they were happy to have me there for the most part. Susy said that

Amy, who was two years younger [than me], and I (who had just turned five) "were so cute together. [Eric's] memory was coming back. I would test him. He loved Tang, and could remember where the Tang was, also some of his favorite soups. I had to wash his head daily—his skull fractures, one was really bad, and I had to keep them clean. I remember crying, trying to hold back tears and not let him see. I really felt that I could get him back to physical health, but the emotional part worried me. The effect of that stayed with him for years. I didn't know how we'd deal with that. He had physical therapy every day with a wonderful therapist, doing his exercises. He [had been] right-handed, but that side was affected. As time went on, we had to teach him how to [be left-handed] and write and walk. He got better so quickly. It was hard on him, he would have to think about what he wanted to say, got confused and frustrated, but sometimes he would blurt something out plain as day."

The influence Richard had on me didn't go away after the murder and my recovery. Even though Richard wasn't around me anymore, I was "still a little monster," according to Lisa. Susy felt that because Richard wasn't an influence any longer, I didn't act [out] that much, but she was around me every day and may have gotten used to it. Lisa saw me less, probably saw my behavior as less acceptable.

"Eric was very smart," Lisa said. "He started kindergarten walking and talking. He had a little trouble printing," which, I suppose, wasn't too surprising since I was four or five at the time and not left-handed, but from what I heard, I had a little more trouble than the other kids. That may have been my injuries in general, but eventually I did learn to write.

"He had a good childhood," according to Susy. "One time, he was in the backyard laying on the ground near the swing-set looking up at the sky and talking. I asked him, 'Who are you talking to?' 'My mom.' It killed me. He had never mentioned her before. I asked him if he wanted to talk about his mom. He said, 'Yes.' They had told us not to mention Paula, but that was a mistake, [the] so-called psychiatrist. So we played it by ear.

As he got older, his behavior got worse again. He saw a counselor who told us to let him talk about whatever he wanted to."

I lived with Susy and her family until I was in 4th grade, so about ten years old, until my grandmother could move from where she was and have me join her. Molly was out of the house by then. I lived with Mary for another eight years, until I graduated high school. My father wasn't really there, just an occasional weekend dad.

Richard hadn't fallen off the face of the earth after I came home. He was in and out of jail because of the murder investigation, but mostly out. And he was still nearby.

The Investigation

The investigation into my mother's murder was botched. There isn't a single person in Muncie who knows the story who doesn't agree with that. Even Mick Alexander believed that. It was one of his excuses for not proceeding with the prosecution of Richard Green. Of course, the police don't want to admit that they made mistakes, but when I spoke to Linda Botkin, who was a detective sergeant in the Muncie Police Department on the night Paula was killed, and later the Assistant Chief of Police beginning in late 1979, she was the first to point out that mistakes had been made. Some of them may have been made to deliberately benefit Richard, but I cannot prove that. I'm not inside anyone's heads, and cannot say what anyone's motivations were. I can only report what happened. And sometimes, actions speak louder than words.

My publisher knows an FBI agent from Louisville, Kentucky—Dr. Don Redden, who is the brother of the polygraph expert I mentioned before—who knows the Louisville-Cincinnati-Indianapolis area pretty well, having grown up in Louisville and been stationed in Cincinnati for a while. When asked about proving corruption, the first words out of Dr. Redden's mouth was that it's extremely difficult to prove. Most of the time, it's something else, something less evil. More often than you'd think, it is just the slow wheels of progress of an investigation that look a lot like law enforcement isn't doing its job. People get frustrated and think there must be a reason other than the rules of evidence why someone isn't prosecuted, or isn't put in prison, or whatever. It must be corruption. Someone knows someone, and the fix is in. Most of the time, Dr. Redden says, it isn't that.

One thing I should point out is that the reason everyone is so upset about Richard not being prosecuted is that everyone, including the police at one time, feel that there was enough evidence to take this to trial. No one says Richard must be convicted. That's for a jury—or at least a judge—to decide. But that's precisely the point. There was enough evidence to take this to trial. If a jury decided to acquit, well, that's how the American justice system works. But all the evidence against Richard would be part of the public record, and at least I'd know what the police know. With that evidence in hand, whether Richard was convicted or not, I would have the opportunity to sue Richard in civil court for wrongful death or something like that. I could still do that, I suppose, but without knowing what the police know, it would be really hard to make that case. This is especially true since Richard has the complete case file, and anything I got wrong he could use to his advantage.

Richard kept insisting that he would never be prosecuted for the murder of my mother, and he wasn't. He reportedly said that the reason he would never go to trial is that he knew all the cops, knew powerful people, and more importantly, he would blow the whistle on a bunch of illegal stuff that was going on that the powerful people in Muncie didn't want out in public. And guess what? He was never prosecuted. The case against him effectively went away. That's what's so infuriating for me and my family. Not that he was never convicted— although we would like to have seen that too— but that he was never even taken to trial. There's no good reason for that. But there are some bad reasons.

There are three possible reasons my mother's investigation was botched and never prosecuted. The first is corruption. Another is the Good Ole Boys network, which in many cases can appear as corruption. And the third is plain old incompetence. It could have been all three. There's really no way to know. It's very difficult to piece together what happened during the investigation without considering one or more of these possibilities, so I will talk about each of them.

Corruption

Let's start with the corruption. A good definition of corruption in government—I got the definition from Transparency International, but I paraphrased it here—is dishonest behavior, including bribery, flaunting or ignoring the rule of law, favoritism especially to criminals or those accused of criminal behavior, and self-serving behavior, including but not limited to embezzlement or making a gift of public funds. The people of Muncie know it has a history of corruption. It's still called "Little Chicago" for its involvement with criminal activity that didn't start with John Dillinger in 1933, and didn't end with the arrest of Muncie Mayor Dennis Tyler and seven other people in 2020 for accepting bribes. I wish I could offer something in the way of verifiable proof of corruption involving my mother's case, but as I pointed out before, proving corruption—conclusively—is very difficult.

Since 1979, there have been arrests and government probes into corruption in Muncie. Even Mick Alexander was accused of corruption at least once. On February 28, 2008, Alexander was arrested, along with another man, by the FBI on bribery charges. Specifically, Alexander was charged with conspiracy to commit bribery, a Class C felony, when it was alleged that he and the other man attempted to get several witnesses to change or withhold their testimony in a case involving a gun. I grew up hearing the stories that if you were in trouble with the law, all you needed to do was give Mick Alexander $10,000, and the charges would go away. This is just a rumor, of course, but it matches with what we saw with Richard Green. His charges did indeed go away. There's no way that a corrupt prosecutor could stay in office unless he had relationships with people who wanted to keep him there, who didn't have a problem with his connections to powerful people, both among the Muncie elite and with the Teamsters, who at that time were well known to be corrupt.

According to a newspaper article in the Muncie Evening Press on April 9, 1980, Mick Alexander was elected to the office of County Prosecutor in November 1978, which would mean he was only four or five months on the job when my mother was murdered. The article goes on to state that Mick had instituted a "no-plea bargaining" policy on felonies, and that "nearly three times as many convicted felons went to prison in 1979, the first year Alexander took office." This policy was bolstered by the presence of four Muncie police officers placed in Alexander's office by Police Chief Richard Heath. The article I'm referencing refers to a feud between Alexander and Chief of Police Gene Hayden, who had taken office in November 1979. Hayden wanted to pull the four police officers and replace them with a police captain. Because of that feud, Alexander began requiring the Muncie PD to file proper forms before he would even prosecute a case. This may have been made worse by Deputy Chief of Police Linda Botkin's investigation into corruption in Delaware County—where Muncie is—which was possibly prompted by Mick Alexander's decision to not prosecute Richard Green for Paula's murder, but of course we don't know, and Mick isn't talking.

Linda Botkin was the first female Deputy Chief of Police in Indiana when she took that position in the Muncie Police Department at the end of 1979. At the time of Paula's murder, Linda was a detective sergeant in the Muncie police, and her partner, Dwayne Cougill, had Paula's case. According to Linda, Dwayne was "obsessed every day" with Paula's murder.

"He had it all wrapped up, took it to the prosecutor, and they just blew it off," Linda said. "I worked with him for about six or seven months, hearing about this every day, day after day. Then, at the end of 1979, I was appointed Deputy Chief. All the officers and all the investigations fell under me. So Paula's murder was the first thing on my agenda. I said, 'As soon as I get in the chief's office, we are going to open an exploration into corruption.' Why aren't they prosecuting Richard? There's enough evidence, way more than enough evidence.

"We started investigating, and when we did, that's when we realized what a mess Muncie is, the corruption in Muncie. The prosecutor, the deputy prosecutor, judges, and attorneys were all involved in flying—they had their own airplane flying drugs. They were going down to Jamaica and Florida. We started an investigation and I just had a handful of men that I could trust. The prosecutor, Mick Alexander, was well liked, and no one wanted to see him go down for anything. So if they [Alexander's allies] got even a bit of information, they'd run to him."

I've done everything I can to corroborate the story about the plane flying drugs. I couldn't find a newspaper article or any other information that would back this up. Which is unfortunate because it would have really put a nail in Mick Alexander's coffin.

The Chief of Police at the time Linda was Deputy Chief was a man named Gene Hayden, who replaced Richard Heath, the Chief of Police at the time of Paula's murder. Linda said of him, "He was honest as can be. But he had, I'll say, a habit of talking too much. And so a lot of times we would not let him know [about our investigations].

"As we got deeper into the [Paula Garrett] investigation, we realized we were going to have to get the feds in. [FBI Agent] Roy Mitchell was the Agent in Charge of the Muncie area. We started working really closely with him. We really thought we were getting somewhere and for some reason we kept getting feedback that they were hearing about our investigation, of what was going on in the investigation."

I asked, "Who is 'They'?"

Linda said, "The prosecutor [Mick Alexander] and the judge. They were hearing about [the investigation]. I had death threats. They were gonna come and kill all my animals [Linda and her husband lived on a farm at that time]. They were going to blow our cars up. They shot at [my partner at the time] early one morning as he left his house, but hit his car, went through, just missed his wife. He was taking her to work.

"We kept thinking, where is this coming from? We kept pulling our little circle tighter and tighter and thinking so-and-so must be telling something. I had the men in the intelligence division, I pulled them in because I thought they were trustworthy and they were, and I thought, we'll get this going. Come to find out it was Roy Mitchell, the FBI guy, was taking the information back to [Mick Alexander and the others]. I sent a man out to get digging through the trash of the prosecutor, and that looked real good for a while, but all of a sudden there was no more trash. Well, Roy had told him we were sending them out at like five in the morning to pick through the trash. During that time we found out all kinds of ways that they were laundering money. They were giving addresses and fake businesses and we'd go there, and it'd be a vacant house or there wouldn't be any house at all. So we knew that they were into something big. We didn't know at the time it was drugs."

When asked what happened to Roy Mitchell, Linda said, "He ended up getting fired." When asked if he was prosecuted, she said, "Oh, no, no, no." We did some research on FBI Agent Roy Mitchell. He was not fired. To the best of our ability to determine, he retired in 1985. What that means is anyone's guess.

At one point, a grand jury was called regarding Paula's murder. Linda was called to testify. Linda said, "the questions they asked me in the grand jury had nothing to do with the murder of Paula Garrett. It was supposed to be for that, but it wasn't. It was just a big smokescreen. And of course, you're forbidden to tell anything that goes on in a grand jury. So they could do anything they wanted in that grand jury. But the questions they asked me had nothing to do with [Paula]. [They involved] the investigation we were conducting [into corruption]. I think what it was, they were fishing, trying to find out exactly what we knew. So they used that as a tool. And then they sued us. You can see that in the Muncie Paper."

When asked if the police department was sued, Linda said, "No, three of us, I believe. Three or four of us that were on that investigation. I think it was $10 million. It was unbelievable. [They were trying to intimidate us.] And they did something different every day. [And then the case against Linda and the others] just disappeared. It was just an intimidation. But I'll tell you, it scared us. The things I had in my name I put them over in my husband's name. We really thought [something bad] was going to happen.

"See, Richard Green who killed Paula Garrett knew all about this [the corruption] and was going to blow the whistle if he got arrested. He was going to blow the whistle on the whole bunch. So they were going to protect him at whatever cost and they did."

When asked, "How can you tell the difference between corruption, incompetence, and laziness?" Linda said, "With Mick Alexander and his crew running drugs and taking bribes and making threats and intimidating and stuff like that, that's corruption."

Linda added, "My partner, Phil Branson, [was] honest as the day is long. He was so into this corruption [investigation]. We arrested an older man, he was probably about 60 years old and his name was Whitey. He was going to blow the whistle on some of the corruption and he told us that there were guns being traded for drugs in Cuba—gun shops and stuff being broken into and stolen—and where the drugs would be. So we asked, 'Who's the big person in the drugs here in Muncie?' He would start crying and shaking every time we'd ask him that question. He kept saying, 'It's so big, so big.' That's all he would say. He would just shake and start crying if we pushed him any further.

"[One day,] I invited [Eric] out [to my house] and he was sitting right there on the hearth and he said something about when [Richard] flipped on the light, [Eric] could see it was Green. I said, 'What? That's never been in evidence!' Then I said, 'We're going to the prosecutor. This is new evidence.' So I took [Eric] up to talk to [Jeffrey] Arnold [the prosecutor in 2013] and said, 'it should be reopened. The case should be reopened.'" The case was still open but it wasn't being investigated. And reinvestigation "never happened," according to Linda.

Let's back up. I've already said that my Uncle Donnie, a Muncie police officer, videotaped an interview with me in 1979 where I said Richard was the one I saw. The interview was in the The Star Press on May 24, 1979, just shy of two months after the murder. Linda was intimately familiar with the evidence the police had. It bothers me, and it should bother you, that she had never seen that videotape or knew of its existence.

The Good Ole Boy's Network

Then there's the Good Ole Boy network. This is probably not a very polite way of describing this, but it's a good one. This refers the preference of people in power to work with people they know and trust, even if those people aren't professional or experienced. It also means that if you're dealing with people you serve, you give preferential treatment to people you know—family, loyal friends—and those who are not in that group get treated differently. Not necessarily worse, just differently. When we were doing research for this book, we came across another book written about how the police in Cleveland functioned in 1922 or so (the title is *Criminal Justice in Cleveland* by the Cleveland Foundation). The people writing the book were outside the network, and they were against how Cleveland was operating. The authors were looking for professional law enforcement officers who were educated, knew their jobs and the law, and treated all the suspects and criminals equally. What they found was a police department run by an administration that valued loyalty and relationships, and that's how they hired people and how they treated the criminals. If you were family, you got a job. If you were a criminal who knew the police, you might be let go when someone else who isn't part of the loyalty structure may go straight to court and straight to prison. This kind of system reinforces respect and staying connected over things like professionalism and the law.

It may sound like I'm saying one is good and one is bad. That's not my point. What I'm saying is, if you're in a system run by the Good Ole Boys network, if you have a relationship with the police, you get preferential treatment where someone who doesn't won't. Richard Green knew the police. He was friends with many of them. To this day, he has coffee every day with some retired police officers. He was very good at working his relationships with those who held power over him. If you value those relationships over the law, then you may not think there's anything wrong with that. I do. I want justice for my mother and for myself, and I don't give a damn about who Richard Green knows, what his relationships with those people are, and who owes who what. You shouldn't be able to get away with murder just because you're friends with the police, or a judge, or the sheriff, or whoever Richard is or was friends with. Mick Alexander comes to mind.

But let's talk this through. Even if Mick Alexander had never heard of or met Richard before the murder, that doesn't mean that the reach of their relationships didn't intersect somewhere.

Richard was in the construction business. He ran backhoes and cranes. That meant he had connections with the Teamsters Union. No matter what is true today, back in 1979, the Teamsters were run like an organized crime organization, especially in Muncie. Being in good with the Teamsters meant Richard had some powerful relationships.

The Teamsters at that time were a strong political force in Muncie. If you wanted to be elected, then you had to be friendly with the Teamsters. Mick Alexander's campaign was approved and funded by John Neal, who was president of the Teamsters Union Local 135 and who, to this day, is still heavily involved, according to my Uncle Ron. Neal was also a heavily involved Democrat—the same party as Mick Alexander—

and Ron told me that "The one office he always controlled was the prosecutor's office. The prosecutor was the one guy in the county no one could touch. The prosecutor had more power than people realize. He doesn't have to prosecute people if he doesn't want to." Which sounds very familiar, doesn't it?

Another player in the Teamsters was a "business manager" named Arthur Hicks, Jr., who everyone knows as Junior Hicks. He was a tough guy for the Teamsters, getting people to sign contracts and stuff. He also happened to be Richard Green's best friend. In order to be elected, Mick Alexander needed to be approved by both John Neal and Junior Hicks.

John Neal recently got busted by the FBI for running illegal gambling machines, "one-armed bandits," in the bars that he and his daughter owned. My Uncle Ron said, "He went to prison, federal prison. [John Neal] wound up getting all these bars. He bought a bunch of them all over Madison County, Delaware County, Randolph County; twenty, thirty bars. He had someone running them, and he put [in] these gambling machines, one-armed bandits they call it. Those are illegal in the state of Indiana." Ron thought the machines were right out in the open, which I remember they were, because I've seen them. They were worth millions to Neal, and operating them meant he would be looking at multiple felonies if caught—actually over 70 Class D felonies, it turns out. "He had them [the gambling machines] for years. Finally the feds stepped in…. He had to spend time in federal prison. Not that many years [in prison], but a while."

I looked up the newspaper accounts of this story, which took place in 2006. According to articles in the NWI Times, Madison County Prosecutor Rodney Cummings called John Neal "the most prolific organized crime figure in the history of our state. This man has enough money that he tends to corrupt local officials."

The article goes on to say, "The arrest came about 1.5 years after Neal's release from the U.S. Penitentiary in Terre Haute. In May 2000 he pleaded guilty in U.S. District Court in Indianapolis to illegal gambling, money laundering and tax charges, admitting an illegal gambling business that he and his wife, Cleo, had operated from Muncie." Which is to say, he went to prison for a year and a half for promoting gambling, but his illegal gambling operation never stopped or missed a beat. The charges in 2006 came *after* he served time in Terre Haute. And it turns out that he plead guilty to "promoting professional gambling," and in exchange for the plea, they dropped the 70 other charges and gave him 18 months of probation.

In 1996, Neal resigned as president of both the Indiana Conference of Teamsters and Teamsters Local 135 in Indianapolis.

There is one more complicating factor in all of this. In the 2000 case against John Neal, Mick Alexander was listed as an expert witness for the defense. The government objected to his status as an expert witness in this case, because he really didn't have any expert knowledge of gambling machines. They felt he was there as a character witness under the guise of an expert witness. As far as I can tell, Mick Alexander never testified as an expert witness in that case. But it's interesting that he was listed.

There's one more thing that is interesting but to be candid I don't really understand what it all means. In the 2000 case against John Neal, Mick Alexander was acting as his attorney as far as I can tell. Richard Reed, who was Mick's Deputy Prosecutor and was in 2000 the prosecutor of Delaware County, apparently prosecuted a case against some people named Wilson, who were acquitted of their charges. When Reed interviewed the jury for the Wilson case, they told him they believed that the gambling machines were "games of skill" and therefore didn't fall under the gambling laws. Reed went to John Neal and his buddies and told them that he wouldn't prosecute bar owners for the use of these gambling machines. He told them he wouldn't prosecute, and they were free to install the machines. These are the same machines that John Neal spent 18 months in jail for. You can look this case up yourself. It's called United States v. Cross, 113 F. Supp. 2d 1253 (S.D. Ind. 2000). Maybe you'll have more luck figuring it out than me.

So, here we have John Neal, called the most prolific organized crime figure in the state's history, who is connected directly to Mick Alexander, who couldn't have been elected without John Neal's okay. Then we have Junior Hicks who is Richard Green's best friend. And we do know that Mick Alexander and Junior Hicks went to visit Richard in jail while he was awaiting prosecution.

There's a lot of reason to believe that Richard was a "heavy" for the Teamsters, or for people they were connected to. My Uncle Ron certainly believes that. After all, there is no question that Richard was a violent psychopath, and it's not surprising that corrupt people or those in the network may need to persuade people *outside* the network to see things their way. I can't say what Richard did and who he did it for. Again, I'm not the police or a prosecutor, and this isn't court. I can't prove what I'm saying, but given all the evidence I can produce, it's likely that this is true. That's my opinion, anyway.

So, if Richard was working as a heavy for the local Teamsters, he would not only have powerful connections but he would *know things*. Important things. Criminal things. Things that the people in power wouldn't want to come to light. After all, the Good Ole Boy's network can only go so far in protecting people from their own actions. Richard himself would often confirm this suspicion, that he knew things. At least one time, probably more, he said that he wouldn't go to prison for my mother's murder because he "knew people" on the "committee." I can't say what committee he was referring to. That's not something I can say or prove. Richard not only counted on those relationships to protect him, but in the end, those relationships *did* protect him.

I should point out that the Teamsters are a diverse organization, and not everyone working for them is corrupt or part of the Good Ole Boy's network, and apart from allegedly covering for Richard, there's really no reason to believe they had any connection to my mother's murder. It wasn't a sanctioned hit, or anything like that. But because Richard was in a position to drop bombs on anyone who *was* corrupt in the Teamsters or the prosecutor's office (or elsewhere), it makes sense that those who had something to lose would look out for Richard.

Incompetence

The third possibility of why things didn't move forward with the prosecution of Richard Green is incompetence. It's possible, even likely, that the police simply messed up the investigation. There was enough evidence at the time that even Mick Alexander initially felt it was open and shut. But, as Jonathan commented, any police officer out of the academy could have closed the case, and any first-year attorney could have prosecuted it and gotten a conviction. So how is it that later Mick Alexander later felt there wasn't sufficient evidence to prosecute Richard? If you give Mick Alexander the benefit of the doubt, and discount corruption and the Good Ole Boys network, how could there not be enough evidence? The only likely explanation is that the police botched the investigation so much that the evidence was unusable.

Dateline, the NBC investigative reporting show, looked into my mother's death for a while. They gave up after some time. Though they didn't say why—it's one of those journalistic things— for a long time, I suspected that it was because the police considered this case open and wouldn't share their evidence. But as I'm researching for this book, I'm beginning to think something else.

I'm beginning to think that this case is just so screwed up they couldn't figure out who to believe.

For example, Linda Botkin reported that Dwayne Cougill, the detective who was her partner at the time of Paula's death, was obsessed with solving the murder. I'd like to take that at face value, but I can't. Here's why. Jonathan reported that when they took Richard Green to the polygraph expert in Chicago, the fix was allegedly in (his opinion, granted, but it was echoed by several others). Two police detectives, who had to have been in on the "fix" if there was one, took Richard there and back again. Those two detectives presumably knew that he "passed" the third polygraph, though as the story goes, they didn't tell Richard. So Richard escapes out the back door of a restaurant when his handcuffs are taken off so he can use the restroom. On August 28, 1979 in the Muncie Evening Press it was reported in two different stories that day that the two detectives who allowed him to escape were named Lt. George Wilson and Detective Sgt. Dwayne Cougill. As in Linda Botkin's partner at the time of the murder.

Here's another disturbing and conflicting piece of information. What it means is anyone's guess. Aaron, one of the main witnesses, got a call threatening him if he testified. At that time, the early 1980s, there was a feature on phones that allowed you to call back the last person to call you, by dialing *69. So Aaron used *69 to call back the person who threatened him. The phone rang in the Southside High School receiving room. At that time, my Uncle Donny (the police officer who interviewed me on video when I said that Richard killed my mother, who is my father Ronnie's brother) worked as a security guard at Southside High School. He still works there. His office is in the receiving room. Make of that what you will.

Let's back up. We need to take a look at what we actually know. We'll start with a timeline following the murder, which took place on March 25, 1979.

- April 11, 1979: The Muncie Evening Press, while reporting on Paula's murder, indicated that part of the evidence from the murder "included 27 bags of blood-soaked articles taken from the murder scene which were sent to the state police lab in Indianapolis for testing. Included were scrapings of flesh and hair taken from the fingernails of the victims *and the suspect*." [Emphasis added.] In the same article, it is reported that "The police investigation of the crime has led to elimination of all suspects but one. But police quickly add that more evidence is needed before any arrests can be made."

- May 3, 1979: Two anonymous businessmen establish a reward fund for evidence that will lead to a conviction. If the reward was not claimed, the money was to be turned over to my family for medical bills and other expenses. No one in my family remembers receiving the money, so I guess that never happened.

- May 10, 1979: Howard E. "Pete" Journay is found murdered, struck no less than 20 times with a blunt instrument, under a bridge in the Mississenewa River. Pete was last seen on April 29 in a tavern in Muncie. May 10 was also my 5th birthday.

- May 15, 1979: 51 days after Paula's murder, Richard Green is taken into custody at my Great Aunt Jane's restaurant.

- May 17, 1979: Richard is arraigned in Superior Court and pleads not guilty to Paula's murder. No charges were brought for my beating, though according to a Muncie Evening Press article on May 16, my attempted murder would be considered "aggravating circumstances" and might increase the length of Richard's sentence if convicted. No charges are brought regarding Pete Journay at any time. That's still an open case as well.

- May 23, 1979: A hearing is held in Superior Court 2, Judge Steven Caldemeyer's court. Richard is denied bail based on

my videotaped interview where I name
Richard and pick him out of a photo
lineup. The videotape was presented to the
court by Mick Alexander. On May 24, The
Star Press reported that Mick stated, "The
case is circumstantial [except] with one
eyewitness.... The weight and credibility
of [Eric's] testimony will be for a jury to
decide." The trial date is set for July 16.
I want to note that I wasn't able to find
any newspaper articles covering the trial on
either July 16 or July 23, which was another
possible date set for trial as reported in the
Evening Press. That's probably because the
trial didn't happen.

- July 21, 1979: Richard's wife Nancy
  offers a $10,000 reward for information
  exonerating Richard. In the Muncie
  Evening Press article on the reward,
  they reported that a Chicago psychic
  was engaged by Richard's family to help
  find exonerating evidence to help with
  Richard's defense. Apparently they gave
  the psychic a police file including photos

taken of Paula at the crime scene. The only thing I can think of to explain how they had the police file is because they obtained it during discovery—the prosecution was required to provide the defense with all their evidence, and apparently that included the crime scene photos and police reports. I've never seen any of that. The Evening Press also reported that (according to Nancy—not a direct quote, mind you) a local psychiatrist who is familiar with Green told them *Green feels guilty that he was unable to prevent Mrs. Garrett's murder.* The guilt feelings make accurate testing of Green impossible, they [presumably the family, not the psychiatrist] claim. [Emphasis added.]

- Somewhere between July 21, 1979 and August 28, 1979: Dr. Roger Caudill of the Meramae Center in Daleville questioned Richard under sodium ambutol (truth serum) and expressed the opinion that Richard didn't kill Paula. Whether you believe truth serums actually induce truth telling or not, it seems like a violation of Richard's Fifth Amendment right not to self-incriminate, but I suppose all that was considered when they gave it to him. Who knows.

- August 26, 1979: Richard is driven to Chicago by Detective Sergeant Dwayne Cougill and Lieutenant George Wilson to submit to a polygraph examination administered by Leonard Harrelson—who was reportedly a college friend of Deputy Prosecutor Richard Reed, Mick Alexander's deputy. According to the Muncie Evening Press (reporting on August 28), during the Chicago polygraph, Richard admitted that he had "struck" Paula in the 24-hour period before the murder. He had not admitted that during the two polygraphs taken in Muncie. Now, this is speculation, but I'm guessing he did that to give plausible deniability to the murder if any evidence of his assaulting my mother were to surface—or if any already existed that we don't know about.

- August 27, 1979: Richard escapes custody from Cougill and Wilson. The detectives and the polygraph examiner Harrelson had gone next door to a café around 6pm to discuss the results. Harrelson and Wilson went inside and Cougill and Richard waited by or in their car. Shortly thereafter, Cougill and Richard go inside, and they sit at the bar (or Richard did, because Cougill reported that he was sitting a few bar stools away from him). As Harrelson was telling Wilson and Cougill that Richard had passed the test, Richard got up to go to the restroom—with permission, without handcuffs—and slipped out the back door (other reports say window). He didn't know he had passed the exam at that time, simply because Harrelson hadn't had a chance to go over the exam with the detectives.

- August 28, 1979: Mick Alexander drops charges against Richard, citing lack of evidence. Mick is quoted in the Evening Press as saying, "Based on all the evidence we have now, I don't think he [Green] did it." That lack of evidence, I should point out, included my testimony, the testimony of multiple witnesses, two failed polygraphs—which are not evidence but the *interviews are*—and, for the record, 27 bags of blood-soaked articles that were sent to the state police lab and never processed—and eventually were lost in a flood that no one remembers. This was the circumstantial case that Mick Alexander decided not to pursue.

- August 29, 1979: Even though the charges were dropped against Richard, Police Chief Richard Heath declared that Richard would remain a suspect. He also said the case was "open" and would remain open until (presumably another) arrest was made in connection with the case. According to the Muncie Evening Press, Heath praised his detectives and insisted that they had investigated the case thoroughly. Which raises the question, what happened with the 27 bags of blood soaked evidence that was never processed and were lost in the flood? (No one I've spoken with will give a timeline for when the flood happened, so it could have been before this for all I know.)

But that's not the end of it all. Sometime in December 1979, after Linda Botkin became Deputy Chief of Police, Mick Alexander asked for a grand jury to investigate what authorities said was "new evidence." This seems to be the report of a jailhouse confession by Richard. He allegedly told convicted murderer Mitchell Waters that he would never go to trial because he "had too much on certain county officials." There was also an allegation that Green had paid $60,000 "to get out of the charge." Linda Botkin investigated this, but wasn't able to find sufficient evidence of the payout. Another thing that was alleged was that there was a conversation between a man named Fred Ginther and the prosecutor's office. Ginther was supposedly an investor in Richard's trucking business. And there was a conversation between Ginther and Leonard Harrelson, the Chicago polygrapher, before the exam took place. I want to make sure it is clear that these things are alleged, not facts, not reported in the newspaper. But so much of this story is alleged, it's hard to tell what to believe.

I'm not sure it's reasonable to believe what was reported in the newspaper either. There was so much that they got wrong about me and my family during the reporting of my mother's case that it makes you wonder what their fact-checking process was. Just as an example, the newspapers reported several times that I was 5 years old at the time of the murder, and that I was living with my father after I got out of the hospital. I was 4 years old on March 25, 1979, and although my father had legal custody of me from the time of the murder, I didn't live with him until much later. Those seem like simple things to check. So even these facts are suspect.

Going back to what we know, or think we know, in February 1980, Deputy Prosecutor Richard Reed said the grand jury (which presumably was the same grand jury as the one in December 1979, which makes sense since it was only about 3 months later) had turned the case over to a countywide homicide investigation. Up until this point, the Muncie (city) Police Department had the case. Mick Alexander and Richard Reed worked for the county. The reason the grand jury turned the case over to the county, Reed said, was because the initial investigation by Muncie PD was "incomplete and one-sided." The grand jurors saw "other possible motivations." Now, whether this finding that the investigation was one-sided was because they were singly focused on Richard Green or because of something else is unclear. During the grand jury, Mayor Alan Wilson was called to testify, presumably to gain the city's cooperation in the countywide investigation, but the city eventually withdrew from the countywide team. No indictments were ever issued from the grand jury.

So here are our choices. 1) Someone paid off Mick Alexander to make Richard Green's case go away (corruption). 2) No one needed to pay off Mick Alexander because he was already beholden to John Neal and Junior Hicks, and they wanted this case to go away (Good Ole Boy's network). Or 3) the cops botched the case so badly that

Mick Alexander couldn't proceed. Personally, I think it was a combination of all three, but short of having actual proof, we're left guessing. This is my opinion, but with all the stories I have, I think it's an informed guess.

There's a fourth possibility. Someone else did it, and all of this is wrong. Even though I was there and saw Richard come into the room that night, even though I picked him out of the photo lineup and named him, there is still some possibility that a stranger came into our house and beat me and killed Paula, and that stranger has never been identified. Yes, it's possible. But that would be a heck of a coincidence if it did happen at that exact moment in Paula's life.

I'm not sure where this fits in this story, but I want to add that Jim Gillum, one of the Muncie detectives working Paula's case, told me that Alexander asked Gillum and Cougill to make a timeline of the murder. He said, if you make a timeline, then it's all done, that's what we're missing. So they put in all this effort to get the timeline right. While they were investigating, they discovered that Richard's wife, Nancy, had gone to the library and checked out books on subjects like how to defeat a polygraph as well as a true story of a girl who was 4 or 5 years old and had a similar story to mine, and what she remembered. That in itself is interesting. So Gillum and Cougill get the timeline down to an accuracy of a few minutes. They brought it up to Alexander's office. Judge Caldameyer—the presiding judge on Richard's case—was there talking to Alexander. When Alexander took a look at the timeline, he told them he decided he wasn't going to prosecute. Well, Judge Caldameyer went ballistic. He said, 'Prosecute this guy!' But of course Alexander never did.

I'm going to say it again. There was enough evidence to go to trial. Was there enough evidence to win? Probably, but I don't know that. I also want to repeat that Mick Alexander instituted a no-plea bargain rule when he took over as prosecutor right before the murder. His conviction rate went up three times. Mick Alexander knew how to win cases when he wanted to. So the question becomes, Why didn't he want to prosecute and win this case?

The Aftermath

When I got out of the hospital, I lived with my Aunt Susy, Uncle Ron, and their two daughters, my cousins. If you ask my family, they'll tell you that I was still a handful, still trouble. Susy said, "[Eric] wouldn't mind me or Ron. Things were getting out of hand. [Eric] was pretty aggressive with Amy [my younger cousin]. I was calling the pediatrician every other day, we were in and out of his office all the time. [Eric] had a lot of ear trouble, but it wasn't just that, it was his behavior. The doctor said, 'your kids have to come first.' It was affecting Amy really bad. I was exhausted, at my end. We didn't know what else to do, so we switched [Eric] over to [Mary]. It killed me, another change for him."

In fourth grade, I moved in with my grandma, Mary. They didn't want me to change schools, so they had to wait until Mary could sell her house and move to Yorktown, where Susy and Ron were living. My father, Ronnie, just wasn't up to taking care of me. Whether that was on account of me being so much trouble or just him not being exactly the fatherly type, it's hard to say. (I did stay with him for a semester when I was in high school, but it didn't work out, and I went back to my grandma's.)

Up until her move when I was in 4th grade, my grandma was still living in the house across the street from where my mother was murdered. I didn't have courage to ask her what it was like living across the street where her daughter was killed. I'm not sure I want to know the answer. Mary was still working between 1979 and 1985 or so when I lived with her. I had stayed with her on and off for those first few years, but it was really hard on her because she had to be at Jane's restaurant at 5:30 or 6am, and she was across town from Ron and Susy, so in order to get me to school and her to work, we had to get up at 4am and leave the house by 5am to make all this work. And since I was so difficult, it was a major operation. It was just easier for me to stay with my aunt and uncle. Except it wasn't, because I was such a problem. No one knew what to do with me.

Having said that, I want to tell you my experience of childhood was great. I couldn't have asked for a better life, except if my mom had lived of course. I owe Susy, Ron, and particularly my grandmother a whole lot.

I want to finish telling a story here. Right after the murder, in 1979, Ron and Susy had just moved back from Ohio and had moved into a new subdivision called Westbrook in an area called Yorktown, an unincorporated suburb of Muncie, a little west of town. It was a nice neighborhood. For some reason, they needed to tear up the streets to replace the sewers. Guess who got the contract. Right, Richard Green.

According to Ron, "After he got out of jail, Richard started working for this other thug. They were partners. The other guy's name was Fred Ginther." I mentioned Ginther earlier, calling him an investor in Richard's trucking business. That's not entirely accurate. From what I understand, Fred Ginther owned the trucks. They just put Richard's name on them, and Ginther and Richard were partners. "[Ginther] is dead now," my uncle explained. "He was a wrestler, a badass. He had a collection agency called Atlas Collections, and all the doctors in town used him. Now, Richard was working at a meat packing plant for a while, which was owned by a guy named Hartmeyer. And Fred Ginther wound up marrying Hartmeyer's daughter. The Hartmeyers were very wealthy, they were from Chicago. The daughter's name was Jane. She's still living. Linda [Botkin] told me about him, because I didn't know him. I asked Linda who he was, and she said 'well, he owns all the thugs in Muncie.' Anyway, Hartmeyer is rumored to have hated his son in law, Fred Ginther. And that's who Richard was partners with when the sewer project came up. They had maybe twenty or thirty trucks, and they all said RW Green. Well, Green didn't have any big money to put on that, it was all Ginther. They put his name on it, but it didn't mean nothing, because it was Ginther."

What it did mean was that right outside the house where I was living right after being almost killed by Richard Green were a ton of trucks with Richard Green's name on them. It was like a gigantic "Fuck you, kid!" Actually, it wasn't, because I was too young to remember it. But, personally, I want to believe it was that, plus I think the "powers that be" wanted my Uncle Ron to do something to Richard. Everyone expected him to. Ron was not a big guy, but he wasn't someone anyone was willing to mess with, even Richard. If Ron killed him, that would solve everyone's problems—at least, the problems of the people who were covering for Richard. Not so much for me and my family, because I can guarantee that Mick Alexander and Richard Reed would have prosecuted Ron as far and as hard as they could, so they could seem tough on murderers.

Ron said, "I went out and checked with a couple of them workers out there. I asked who had the contract, who RW Green was. And they told me it was same 'Dick Green' who had just been released from jail."

Since he was running trucks, it had to be union, and it had to be Teamsters. So there's another connection between Richard, John Neal, and Junior Hicks, and now Fred Ginther was part of the connection too. I'm going to remind you that Ginther had spoken with the polygrapher in Chicago, Leonard Harrelson, who they took Richard to, who passed him. That may not mean anything, but really, it probably does.

I wanted to know what happened to all those trucks after the contract was up and the sewers laid. Uncle Ron told me that they ended up being sent to Kentucky and sold.

While the RW Green trucks were right outside our house, Ron told the workers that if Richard came on his property, he would be "dead meat." According to Ron, "A couple of days later, Stonebreaker [who was an investigator for the prosecutor's office] called my boss and said that [my boss and I] should get up to the prosecutor's office right away. When my boss told me that, I said, 'I'm not going anywhere.' I went out to the phone booth and called Linda [Botkin]. She hit the roof—God, she hit the roof. She told me not to go out there, no matter what. And I never did. They dropped that pretty damned quick. And then it was a few days later, it was in the paper that I threatened Green. That's the reason they called. [Linda] thought it was funny at the time."

Ron lost his job at Pepsi because of the murders, too. Right after the murder, he was at the police station every day, looking for answers. He was there so often that after a while he stopped going to work. Personally, I feel it's a shame he did that, for all the results he got. But he was dedicated to getting justice for my mother and me, and for that I am eternally grateful.

Another interesting thing that happened was when Richard's defense attorney, a man named Donald H. Dunnuck sent Ron a message that Richard's brother Terry wanted to talk to him. Terry wanted Ron to come out to the junkyard where he worked to talk. Well, Ron wasn't anyone's fool, so he waited a while. He also made sure he had someone with him, and a gun. After almost a month, he went out to the junkyard to talk to Terry finally, but he wasn't there. "So I asked this guy who was there, 'Who is this Terry

Green?' Here's how he described [Terry]: 'You know that guy that's in jail for killing that woman and beating that boy?' I said, 'Richard Green?' He said, 'Yeah, [Terry] is his brother.' And I said, 'Oh, where's he at now?' And he said, 'He's not here today. He's in jail.'

"So I went to the police and asked what Terry was doing in jail. And I found out that he hung himself in jail. I asked, 'What was he in jail for?' And the cop said, 'He stole his brother's truck.' 'Which brother?' And the cop says, 'Dick Green.'"

I'm going to repeat that to make sure we all have this right. At the age of 25, Terry Green died on April 22, 1980 in jail of an apparent suicide while awaiting trial on charges that he stole a truck from his brother Richard. Kinda makes you wonder what Terry wanted to tell Ron. Was he going to give Ron evidence against Richard? Or was he going to try to kill Ron? Or something else? I don't know. But none of us will ever know, because Terry's dead.

The police officer who told Ron about Terry's death was Dwayne Cougill. Jim Gilliam was another police officer in the Muncie PD, and at one time Cougill's partner. (I'm wondering how all these cops all call each other their partners, whether that's literally true or just shorthand for the fact that they all worked together.) He told Ron that "Cougill and Green were buddies."

My school life was nothing like my mother's. I don't know where all the smart genes went, but if I got them, I didn't know it. Mary tells me that the problem wasn't that I couldn't do the work, but that I wouldn't. She would sit with me for hours and help me with my work, and then I would just throw it in my locker and never turn it in. I was too busy socializing. According to Mary, my mother never did anything like that.

In fifth grade, I was getting into trouble. Not like "call the police" trouble, but the story goes that I was running around with some boy my age, and my teacher went to Susy and told her not to let me hang out with him. "[Eric] was very naïve," Mary said. Just like my mother.

I was in trouble with the principal all the time. Especially in high school. For better or worse, my grandma Mary worked at the high school when I was there. She worked in the cafeteria and also sold tickets to the school's sporting events. Whenever I got in trouble for cutting class, she knew about it before I could concoct a convenient story.

One time, my grandma came to my math class and sat down next to me, trying to get me to pay attention, to get my work done. She thought it was embarrassing, but I didn't. I thought it was funny.

I was the class clown in high school. Not bad, but not good. Some people thought I was mischievous, others thought I was a jackass. I thought I was just goofy.

I had trouble with math which had to do with my injuries. They had me tested, and it turned out that the part of my brain that figures numbers was damaged. I can do basic arithmetic, add and subtract, multiply, but I struggle with division. On the other hand, I was good at literature, creative writing, grammar, spelling. As a freshman, I was in English classes with sophomores and juniors, like my mother with her math classes.

I graduated high school in 1992. I had lived with Mary until I was 18 years old, and then again when I was 22 or 23 for a bit. I went to college, but I didn't graduate. I really wanted to get a degree in psychology, maybe counsel people who went through what I did. But college was a lot different from high school. They expect you to work. And for psychology, they expect you to do math. So I was stuck. I liked my psychology classes, but I still tended to skip class.

In February 1996, I had a daughter, Kassidy. She's the light of my life. In 2019, Kassidy had a boy, Kyler. As I write this, I'm 46 years old. I'm on disability, almost exclusively from the injuries I received that night in 1979. It's frustrating for me. If I could do anything I wanted with my life, I would work with people with PTSD from attacks and other assaults, like me. Not necessarily with kids—I wouldn't feel comfortable with that—but I wanted to study psychology so I could be a kind of counselor. I never got very far with that. Not only did Richard Green take my mother, he took my future.

Open Case

I get three hours of sleep on a daily basis. I never could sleep that well, even in high school. It's because of the attack, I'm sure. Really, I'm lucky to get two or three hours of sleep for seven or eight days in a row, then I'll sleep one solid night. After that, I'm back to the insomnia.

I have nightmares every once in a while. It's usually the same thing, the night of the murder. My conscious memory of the murder is very limited, but I think in my subconscious I know a lot more. The nightmare goes something like this. The light comes on, and there's Richard with something in his hand. I'm closer to the door than my mom, and Richard hits me first. I'm sure of that. Richard is jerking me around by my right arm, and just pounding on me. And there's blood everywhere, and a lot of pain.

I do remember my mother screaming. A lot. I don't understand how the people next door, Jonathan, Aaron, and Leslie Ann, could hear all that and think, oh, that's normal.

The screaming bothers me. Actually, all of it bothers me. I think about my mother, at 22 with a 4-year-old child, and she's thinking about me, trying to protect me, and there's nothing she can do about it. Richard was just bulldozing. He was unstoppable.

I hate that her last thought was that she couldn't stop Richard from hurting me. Nobody should die like that. Nobody. People die in airplane accidents, get run over by buses, and that's terrible, but nobody should die feeling helpless, watching someone beat their child.

In 2012, there was a story in the newspapers about the murder again. Jeff Arnold was the prosecutor then. He was quoted as saying "Well, short of a confession, there's nothing we can do." Which is bullshit. Of course Richard is going to read that. Jeff Arnold just handed Richard his life on a silver platter. Richard took my mother's life, took my future, and he's being given a pass by prosecutor after prosecutor for decades. I hate that.

I've dealt with PTSD a lot. I was 4 years old, and there was nothing I could have done about what happened. Still to this day, I am terrified of people with long hair and beards, which is what Richard looked like back then. I'm an adult, I'm not afraid of many people, but if I see someone with long hair and a long beard, he's the one I'm going to keep an eye on.

I have a memory of being 4 years old in Richard's Ford pickup, and I'm sitting in the middle between Richard and my mom waiting in line at a Wendy's drive thru. There's a transmission hump in the middle, and Richard has a cane resting up against the hump. I don't have a clue why he had a cane. Anyway, I accidentally bumped the cane, and it hit the gas pedal. Well, Richard stopped the truck before it hit anything, but he was angry. He pulled his arm back to punch me. Punch a 4-year-old. My mom said, "Don't you dare hit him!" And he didn't. But that's the kind of man we're talking about.

I didn't prove anything in this book. All I have are stories and rumors and 40-year-old memories. The evidence of what happened that night exists. The police have it, the prosecutors have it, and Richard has it. But I don't, and the chances of me ever learning the whole truth of what happened that night and why Richard never faced that truth are almost nonexistent.

There were a couple of attempts at cold case investigations. Melissa Pease, who today is the Deputy Chief of Police in Muncie, worked the case for a while. She took down a lot of information, including the names and phone numbers of my family, and promised to interview them. But after six or seven months, she hadn't called even one of them. I remember the last time I spoke to her, I was yelling at her on the phone. Nothing was happening, and it didn't seem like it ever would.

I shouted, "Just do your job." She never did. And I never got an explanation of why. Now she's Deputy Chief, and she'll probably read this book. And even so, I doubt she'll reach out to me to tell me the truth of what she found. Because this is an open case.

In fact, the only people who have really taken an interest in helping me get the complete story out are my publishers, Steven and Leya Booth. They're friends with a woman who worked for the Muncie PD for years and knew my case. After talking to her, they reached out to me in early 2019 and asked if I wanted to publish a book about the case. Of course I said yes. They flew out from Los Angeles twice now to interview my family and research the case. They talked to almost everyone having to do with the case who is still alive. Except Richard. Leya even offered (Steven would say *threatened*) to come to Muncie and knock on Richard's door and ask him to comment on the case. For better or worse, Steven and I talked her out of it. Richard is now about 77 years old, but he's not someone I would trust not to be violent with her. As I said before, he's not going to confess—which is the only way he'll ever be convicted—so what's the point?

I have to ask myself, what have I accomplished here in publishing this book? Honestly, I'm not sure. As I said in the introduction, I want Richard to have to face justice—whether he is convicted or not—and the people who helped him to be exposed. Did I do that? Probably not. I don't really have a rational expectation that anything will come of this. I suppose someone could twist the book to their own advantage, calling it defamation, and sue me for publishing it. But really, they would have to prove that they lost their reputation and were financially harmed by this book in order to win a case like that. But they wouldn't want to win the case. They would just want to make my life even more miserable for not shutting up about it, and cost me and my publisher a bunch of money for having the balls to try to bring this story out again. In America, you can sue someone for something stupid like that, but I can't sue Richard for beating me and killing my mother. Both ways, I'd be the one who would have to prove I have the truth on my side. But I don't have the truth. All I have are memories and stories and nightmares and pain and screaming.

I also want to make it clear that everything in this book that I cannot prove is my opinion, my belief, and not the opinions or beliefs of my publisher. They're supportive of my search for justice, but this book is on me.

I'm not asking anyone to pity me. I don't really care what you think of me for bringing this book out. What I care about is that my mother's short life will not be forgotten, swept under the rug because someone inconveniently killed her.

My mother deserved more than that. My family deserves it too.

www.ingramcontent.com/pod-product-compliance
Lightning Source LLC
Chambersburg PA
CBHW071233020426
42333CB00015B/1449